POLAR BEAR

BY TYLER GRADY

Dylanna Press

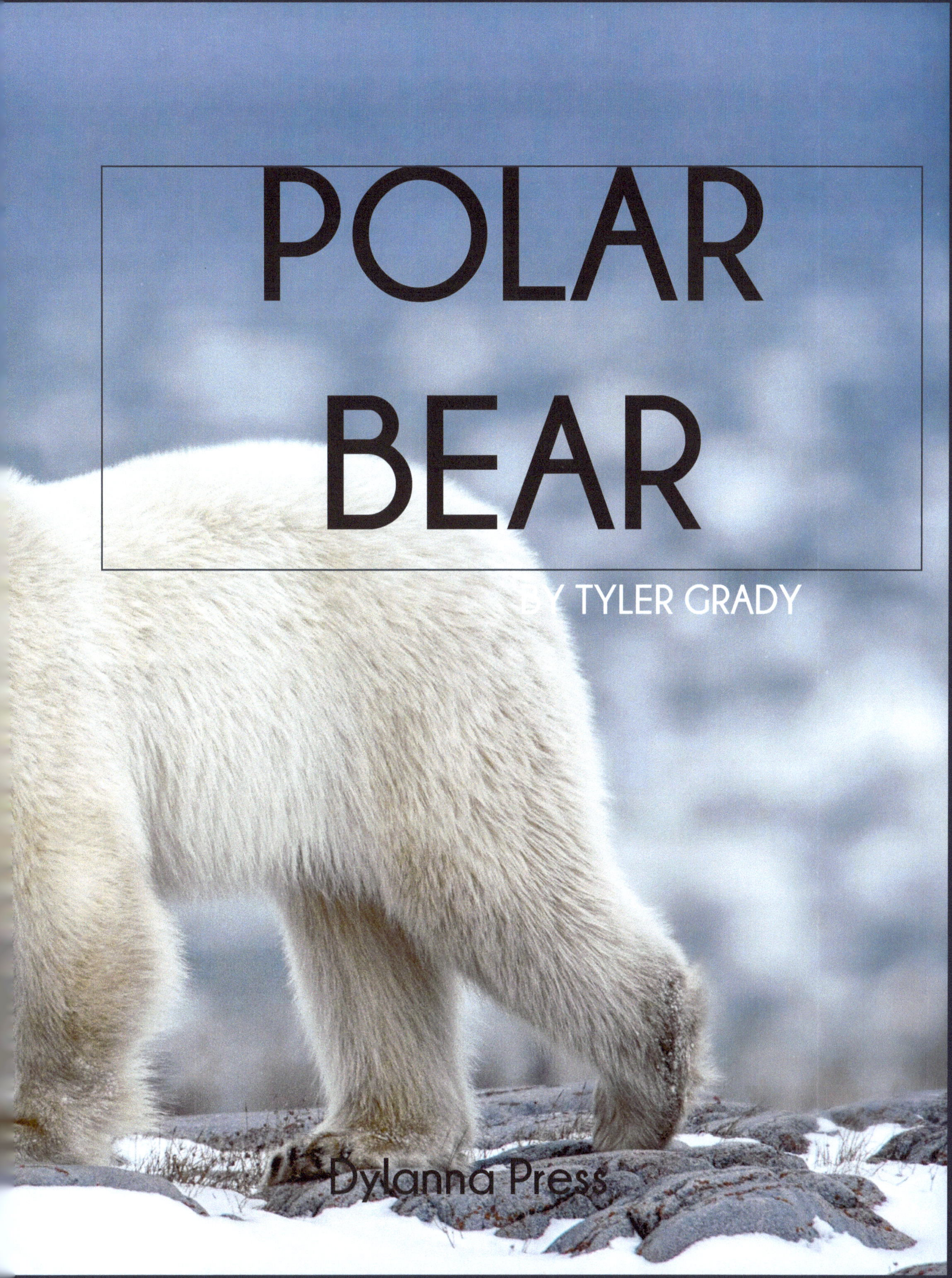

Polar bears can be found in the Arctic, Alaska, Canada, Russia, and Greenland. They are the only member of the bear family that are classified as **marine mammals**. Their lives are spent in and near the sea, dependent on the ocean's health and bounty for their survival.

They are related to other types of bears such and grizzly and brown bears and are part of the Ursidae family. Their scientific name is *Ursus martimus*, meaning sea bear.

_____

marine mammals – warm-blooded animals with hair or fur that give birth to live young and spend most of their time in the ocean

Polar bears are the largest bears in the world, with males weighing between 800 to 1200 pounds (360 to 550 kg) and females weighing from 300 to 700 pounds (135 to 320 kg). They stand about 5 feet (1.5 meters) tall to the shoulder and range in length from 6 to more than 9 feet (1.8 to 2.75 meters).

Polar bears have a stocky build with long necks, small heads and ears, and a short tail. They have muscular limbs and large wide paws. Their skin is black, which absorbs the heat of the sun and their thick fur, while appearing white, is actually **transparent** in color.

---

transparent – a material that allows light to pass through

Polar bears can live in harsh **environments** and severely cold temperatures. As cold as -50 degrees Fahrenheit (-45 degrees Celsius)! They live along the ocean's shore and on the ice sheets that form in the Arctic.

Since polar bears spend much of their lives in the water it is not surprising that they are extremely good swimmers. They are able to swim for long distances and for many hours, even days, at a time. Their large, webbed paws help them to speed through the water and a thick layer of body fat allows them to stay warm in the icy sea.

---

environment – surroundings or conditions in which an animal lives

The polar bear has many physical **adaptations** to its environment.

Their fur is designed for maximum insulation with a short dense layer of underfur and a top layer of varying length hairs. This fur coat, combined with a thick layer of blubber (body fat), provides almost complete protection from the cold.

Their huge paws and sharp claws also help them to survive. Measuring almost 12 inches (30 cm) across, their paws are covered by small bumps on the bottom that provide traction on slippery snow and ice. In addition, their long, sharp claws help them navigate across icy surfaces.

_____

adaptations – ways in which a species becomes fitted into its natural environment to increase its chance of survival

Polar Bears are **carnivores**.

Unlike other species of bears, they do not usually eat any fruits or vegetables.

Seals make up the main part of their diet. They will also scavenge the **carcasses** of dead beluga whales and walruses.

When food is scarce they will eat anything they can find, including fish, rodents, birds, eggs, and even reindeer.

---

carnivore – an animal that only eats meat

carcass – the body of a dead animal

Polar Bears are **nomads** and

will travel long distances to find food. They cover approximately 15 miles per day and have been known to swim more than 100 miles.

The main prey for polar bears is the ringed seal. They use their strong sense of smell to locate seals below the ice and then they wait for them to come to the surface to breathe. They then will bite or grab the seal and pull it onto the ice to eat.

An adult polar bear will eat up to 20 percent of their body weight in food at one time. They eat every 5-7 days.

---

nomads – animals that move from place to place

Female polar bears only mate

about once every three years. Because of this, males have to compete with one another for the available females.

Competition is fierce among males. Polar bears are not **monogamous**, often mating with several females in one season.

Breeding season takes place between March and June. Males seek out females by following their scent, often across long distances.

Once paired up, the polar bears only stay together for about a week before once again going their separate ways. Males will then look for another partner.

_____

monogamous – staying with one mate at a time

Pregnancy lasts about eight

months. During this time, the mother polar bear will build a den to give birth in. She will dig into the snow to form a small cave just large enough for her and her babies.

Polar bear babies are called cubs. A mother bear gives birth to 1-4 cubs, but most commonly two cubs. When polar bear cubs are born they are very small, weighing only about 1 pound (1/2 kg). They are helpless, blind, deaf, and without teeth.

They stay in the den with their mother for several months, not coming out until springtime. The mother bear takes care of her cubs for two to three years. She protects and feeds them, and teaches them how to hunt, swim, and survive on their own.

Polar bears

Polar bears sleep 7-8 hours per day, about the same as humans. They also take several naps throughout the day. They tend to be more active in the morning and less active at night.

They sleep out in the open on top of the snow. Sometimes they will dig in the snow to make a **shallow** pit and then curl up in it to sleep. Only mother bears and her cubs sleep in dens.

_____

shallow – little depth

Polar bears do not **hibernate** in the winter except for pregnant females who stay inside dens. Other adult females and males are active year round and they are well equipped to survive in the harsh winters of the Arctic zone.

Food sources can be unpredictable in the Arctic and polar bears must often survive months without eating.

To prepare for summer when food is **scarce**, they will eat as much as possible in the winter and spring, building up their fat reserves.

_____

hibernate – a dormant or resting state; conserves energy in winter

scarce – difficult to find; not common

Polar bears are generally **solitary** animals. Except for during breeding season and mothers with cubs, they prefer to be alone.

They are not **territorial** and they do not form social groups.

Polar bears do communicate with one another, however. They do this through scent, body language, and **vocalizations**.

They use growls and roars as warnings. Male polar bears locate breeding females through scent. Head wagging from side to side indicates playfulness, while head down and ears back signals an attack may be coming.

_____

solitary – **to be alone**

territorial – to defend a certain area

vocalizations – **the sounds an animal makes**

In the wild the average lifespan of a polar bear is fifteen to eighteen years. They can live up to thirty years in captivity.

It's hard to know the exact **population** of polar bears, but scientists estimate there are currently about 30,000 worldwide.

Due to their declining numbers, they are considered to be a **vulnerable species**.

---

population – the number of particular species

vulnerable species – a species that is likely to be come endangered

Polar bears are at the top of the Arctic food chain. They are **apex predators** and have no natural predators except other polar bears. Adult male polar bears will sometimes kill baby polar bears. Small cubs can also become prey to wolves.

Young polar bears, being less-experienced hunters, as well as older, slower bears, can face the threat of starvation.

Diseases and parasites, such as roundworm, can also sicken and kill polar bears.

However, the biggest threats to polar bears are human related.

_____

apex predators – an animal at the top of the food chain

Polar bears have been hunted by humans for thousands of years for both their fur and meat. Hunting, while regulated by some governments, is still a leading cause of polar bear death.

Climate change is another major threat to polar bears. Rising temperatures and sea levels are impacting the areas where the live. Shrinking sea ice and reduced seal populations make food harder and harder to find.

Pollution, from oil spills and toxic chemicals in the environment, are also negatively affecting polar bear health and their ability to reproduce.

---

climate change – long-term changes in expected weather patterns

Polar bears are beautiful and interesting animals.

Despite living in some of the harshest conditions on Earth, they have been able to adapt and survive.

However, the future for these magnificent animals is uncertain. Faced with dwindling sea ice and increasing temperatures, the threat of **extinction** is real.

_____

extinction – the disappearance of animal from the Earth

Word Search

```
R W C A R N I V O R E I T I Y
A C L I M A T E M U X T H P P
E Z L T Z D A B A K N E U A R
B G R D A X E W Y E M U Z B E
R S Q E X R Y N M C O L D L D
A J W E X E C N W I P S F U A
L E P I R T O T L O E K C B T
O A W P M R I A I I S B S B O
P F O K I M R N C C E J S E R
O H U V S X E E C D A P A R C
S B N R E L P R I T I C C T D
B E B E G S R A I C C X R V T
U M S L A M M A M A E B A D N
C N O I T A T P A D A F C E Z
S S W A P H N O M A D S T C O
```

ADAPTATION	COLD	PAWS
APEX	CUBS	POLAR BEAR
ARCTIC	ENVIRONMENT	PREDATOR
BLUBBER	EXTINCT	PREY
CARCASS	FUR	SEA ICE
CARNIVORE	MAMMALS	SPECIES
CLIMATE	NOMADS	SWIMMER

INDEX

Published by Dylanna Press an imprint of Dylanna Publishing, Inc.
Copyright © 2021 by Dylanna Press
Author: Tyler Grady

Animals

Energy

Plants

Land

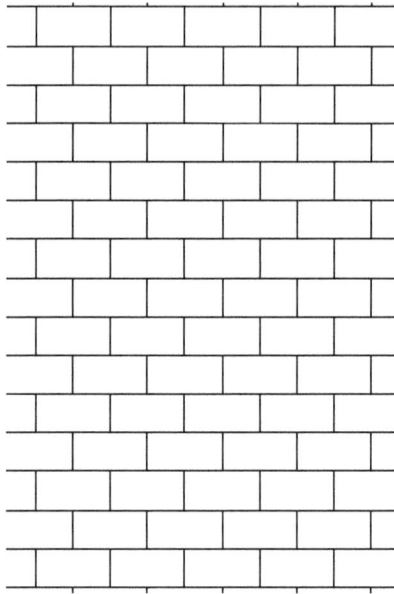

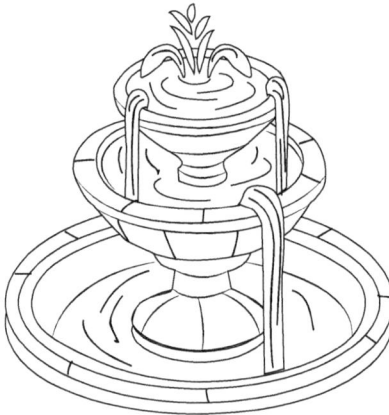

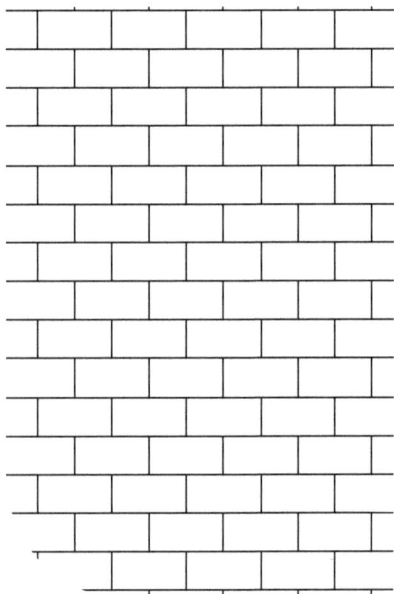

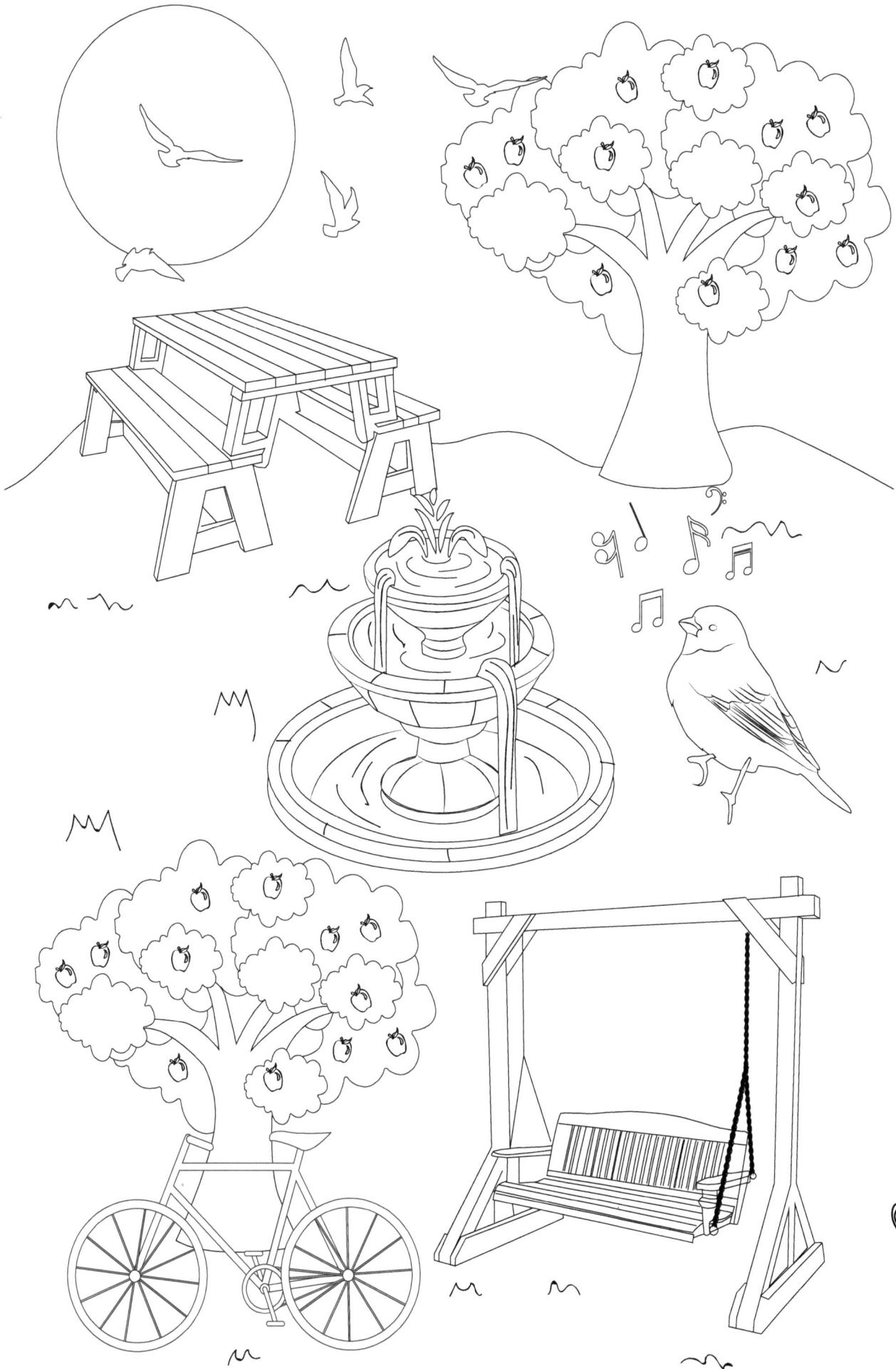

Commons

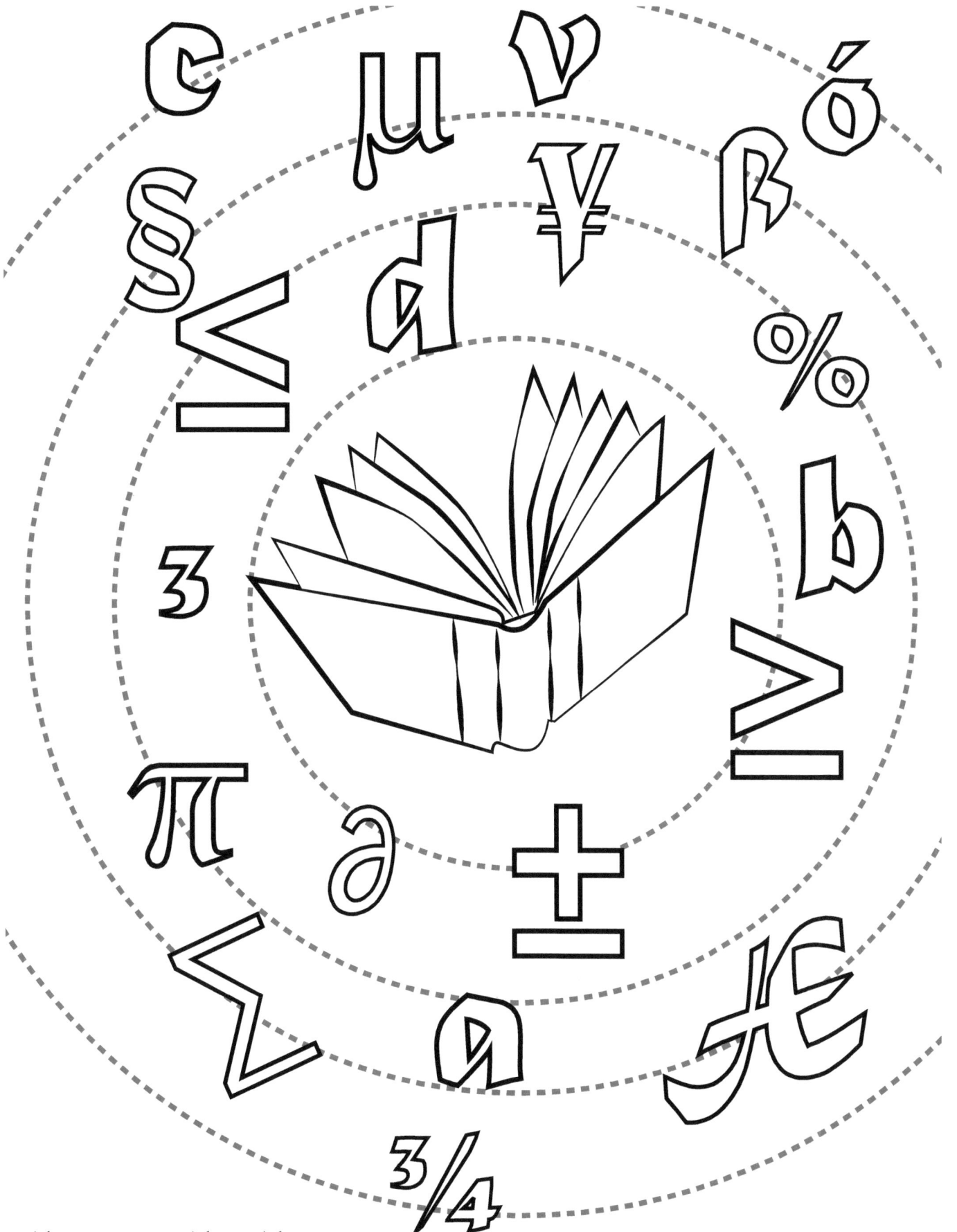

knowledge

water

air

health

rights